Eating gluten-free with Emily a st
E 618.92 KRU   113654

Kruszka,
Ingalls M

D0929251

Eating Gluten-Free with Emily

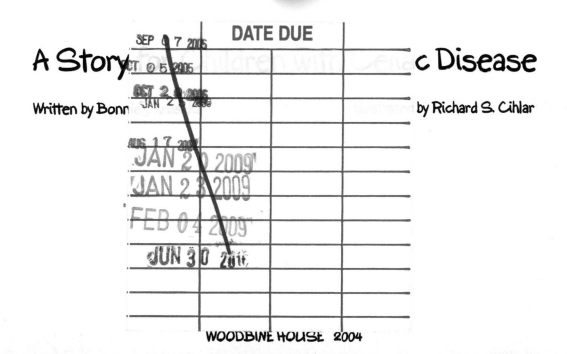

gluten-free
Snack Sack

A Story ~~for children with~~ c Disease

Written by Bonnie   by Richard S. Cihlar

DATE DUE

SEP 0 7 2005
OCT 0 5 2005
OCT 2 8 2005
JAN 2 5 2006
AUG 1 7 200?
JAN 2 0 2009
JAN 2 3 2009
FEB 0 4 2009
JUN 3 0 2010

WOODBINE HOUSE 2004

INGALLS LIBRARY
RINDGE, NH 03461-0224

Hello. My name is Emily.

I like to jump rope, pick flowers, and paint.

I have a dog named Max.

My mom says I am special.
She tells me that oodles of things, added
together, make me so special.

I have freckles. I laugh a lot. I tell good jokes.
And I have celiac disease.

When I was five years old, I was very sick. I had diarrhea.
I was moody. I had a big belly and my clothes did not fit!

So my mom took me to the doctor.

The doctor said I needed some tests, but not the kind I took in school.
He needed to prick my arm to get a few tubes of blood.

Because my body makes new blood every day, the doctor said taking some that day was okay.

It hurt just a little, but the pinch went away faster than I could say, "Purple elephant."

A few days later, the doctor called. My mom said I needed to go to the hospital for more tests. I was scared!

The nurse at the hospital was very nice. She gave me pink pajamas to wear, took my temperature, and held my hand.

INGALLS LIBRARY
RINDGE, NH 03461-0224

The doctor said he was going to look at my belly.
Then he gave me medicine to make me sleep.

When I woke up, the test was done.

That sure was an easy test, and I got lots of balloons.

Later on, my mom told me I have celiac disease.
She said the food that I eat goes on a journey through my body.

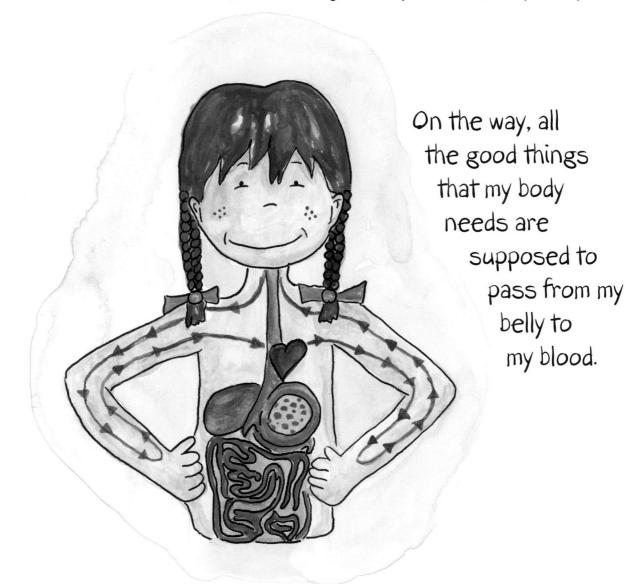

On the way, all
the good things
that my body
needs are
supposed to
pass from my
belly to
my blood.

Because I have celiac disease, my blood
did not get the good stuff and that was why I felt so sick.

My mom said that the disease causes a bad reaction to something called gluten, so my body had a hard time doing its job. That was why the journey from my stomach to my blood was a little messed up. She told me that gluten comes from wheat, barley, and rye.

She said gluten is found in things like . . .

. . . cookies, mac-n-cheese, and PB&J's.

So, I have to eat special foods with no gluten, and now I feel better.

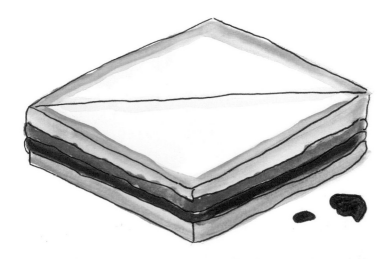

Special foods are not bad, just sometimes different.
I still eat watermelon, yogurt, and chicken. My mom still makes me eat
green beans. YUK! I just eat some foods like cereal,
bread, and pasta that are not made with gluten.

We say the food is "gluten-free."

Now every Saturday, we go to the health food store. My mom buys rice flour, corn flour, and potato flour. I buy animal crackers, cinnamon rolls, and my favorite chocolate brownies. All the stuff is marked gluten-free.

Sometimes at birthday parties, I feel a little weird. My mom bakes me my own gluten-free cupcake because I can't eat birthday cake. I just tell everyone, "To be as healthy as I can be, I need to eat gluten-free!"

After school I like to play at Dylan's house.
Dylan's dad used to forget I have celiac disease.
We reminded him, but one time I had to eat
fruit for dinner, lots of fruit.

So now my mom packs an emergency gluten-free snack sack.

At restaurants, my mom makes a fuss. She takes no chance that gluten gets in my food.

"Hot dog, no bun please . . . . What kind of ketchup? Are your fries fried with anything?"

We say, "We are gluten detectives. Answer the questions, please."

Treats at school are tricky. On bad days, everyone but me gets cookies at snack time, so I grab for my gluten-free snack sack.

On good days, the teacher calls ahead and my mom bakes the same kind of cookies for me, but she uses gluten-free flour.

During my summer vacation, I go to camp. My mom calls the
camp director, Charlie, to plan my special meals.
He always says he will take good care of me,
but my dad packs tons of gluten-free food anyway.

Last year, I made a very big discovery! I am not the only kid who has to pack a gluten-free snack. I met a boy named Nate who has celiac disease just like me! We had all sorts of fun sharing gluten-free s'mores and camp stories. And we've been pals ever since.

Because I have to do some things differently than other kids, having celiac disease isn't always easy. So, when I feel sad or mad or alone, I tell my mom. She always makes me feel better.

She reminds me that celiac disease is only a part of who I am,
and that eating like me, gluten-free, makes me special.
What makes you special?

A Note for Parents of Children with Celiac Disease

Dear Parent,

When I was diagnosed with celiac disease in 1995, I, like most people, had never heard of the disease. I began visiting all of the libraries and bookstores in my area looking for clarity, direction, and hope. In the course of a few weeks, however, I discovered that these resources were sorely limited. I felt lost and alone, but in many ways I managed.

Four years later, following the birth of my son Max, my seemingly manageable "celiac life" became much more complex. At the age of two, Max began having digestive problems. He had many questions about his condition, and my early attempts at the answers were not very helpful.

Eating Gluten-Free with Emily provides many of the answers I wished I'd had at the onset of Max's symptoms. I hope it will provide direction and hope as you and your child begin your lifetime journey with celiac disease.

While the lifestyle changes that a diagnosis of celiac disease brings can at first seem overwhelming, the increased availability of gluten-free products, better food labeling, and growing awareness of celiac disease makes management of a gluten-free diet more workable than ever before. Emily reminds us that celiac disease is only one small part of what makes your child special. And in most other ways, your child is just like any other child!

I wish you and your child the best of health,
Bonnie

INGALLS LIBRARY
RINDGE, NH 03461-0224